SHARE!

One Heart. One Verse. One Hope

A Simple, Single-Verse Gospel Presentation

Dr. Troy Dixon, Pastor
Normandy Park Baptist Church

normandypark.org
troydixon.net

.

DEDICATION

I dedicate this book to the two most passionate witnesses I know: Ronnie Smith and Wayne Brown.

Ronnie is an itinerate evangelist who travels city to city, week by week, preaching the gospel and seeking revival for the church.

Wayne spent years as a Word of Life missionary and now leads his own ministry called Community Impact in Jacksonville, Florida.

These men do not seek to fill quotas, please a denomination, or chase the applause of others. They are consumed with one simple question: "do you know my Jesus?"

God uses them to win the lost. He also uses them to provide an example that humbles and teaches me. They have shaped my life.

ronniesmith.org

communityimpactministries.com

How beautiful upon the mountains are the feel of him who brings good news, who publishes peace, who brings good news of happiness, who publishes salvation, who says to Zion, "Your God reigns." **Isaiah 52:7**

ACKNOWLEDGEMENTS

Thank you to Doug Taylor and Judy Evans for editing SHARE! You took my ramblings and made them coherent. You are good friends and great blessings to my life.

Thank you to Ronnie Smith for helping me with a "theological" read through. I am always reminded that just because it sounds good doesn't mean it is good. Thank you for you assistance.

Table of Contents

INTRODUCTION

Do we need yet another gospel presentation or
evangelism strategy?

There are dozens of these presentations and strategies
available for the church today. Some are brief, while
others are extensive. Some are visual in nature, while
many are verbal. Some presentations begin with the
book of Romans attempting to convict the hearer of
their sin and need of a Savior. Others begin with
creation and God's intention of innocent perfection.
There is a gospel presentation for every single
personality type, environment, and witnessing
opportunity that can be imagined.

Do we REALLY need another? I would say no. But I
would also say yes.

No, we do not need another approach. As previously
stated, there are many quality presentations available.
The Kingdom of God would not suffer any great loss
or setbacks if this particular strategy were not
developed. The church has done well for the past two

millennia without it. We would continue to go forward if it did not exist.

But I would also say, YES! A different strategy can help us reach our neighbors, friends, and families. I believe that an affinity for a particular strategy can be as personal as the shoes we choose. I wear a size 11, and there are a lot of size 11 men in the world. There are millions of size 11 shoes in the world, but not every pair works for every man. A pair that is attractive to me and fits my foot well might not attract or feel right on another man. We need options. SHARE! is another option that I hope is a fit for different people.

The genesis of the SHARE! strategy is a desire to equip believers with a tool that is simple and clear. It is based on one verse. One simple, clear verse (John 5:24) says, or points to, everything that needs to be said regarding our spiritual need and God's provision. One simple, clear verse that can be easily memorized and quoted. The presentation consists of four statements that provide a simple and clear path for a witness to follow as they converse with the one who needs salvation.

The strategy's simplicity is also reflected in the tagline, "One Heart, One Verse, One Hope." One heart does not mean to only share with one person. It means the focus is not on mass evangelism but rather on personal evangelism. The majority of people who come to a saving knowledge of Jesus do so because of the influence of someone they know who cared enough to share the gospel with them. Mass evangelism works and has its place in the church, but it is the exception, not the norm.

One verse, as previously stated, keeps the presentation clear and focused. It can be read to the listener from a Bible or an app. It can easily be written out on a napkin. Once memorized, the witness can quote it in any context. This is "nimble evangelism."

Lastly, there is one hope. That one hope is Jesus. His life, death, burial, and resurrection are not one hope among several options. Jesus is *the* one hope, to the exclusion of all the others the that world religions might offer in His place.

This book began as an intellectual exercise to satisfy my desire to share the gospel from one verse. I found a great single-verse presentation that did not quite fit me—remember the shoe metaphor—and it sent me searching the scriptures for a different verse that suited the need. Once I stumbled upon John 5:24, I began to work on the presentation. Then my equipping role as a pastor-teacher (Ephesian 4:11) kicked in, and I began to think of several other resources that would benefit a believer who is serious about being an intentional witness. Before long, a small book was taking form.

In addition to the actual presentation, I added some notes on strategy. The notes point to truths that are important when presenting the gospel and led to the addition of some aids on how to "live as an evangelist," seeking opportunities to share. There is also a guide for connecting with people through prayer and some open-ended questions that allow them to share their stories. Tools for preparing a salvation testimony, praying for a lost friend, and how to guide a new believer to growth and maturity are also included. Having made many blunders when sharing the gospel, I included some gaffes and mistakes to avoid. The book ends with a glossary of terms related to evangelism and the scriptural support for the SHARE! presentation.

As brief as it is this book is a toolbox to equip believers to be faithful witnesses for Jesus Christ. But, ultimately, success is not found in a book. Success is not in sensing the need or making a commitment. It's not even in being equipped for the task. Success as a witness is when we actually SHARE!

1

THE PRESENTATION

May I share with you one verse of scripture which promises that FAITH in Jesus brings FREEDOM from judgment and life FOREVER?

John 5:24 says, "Truly truly, I say to you, whoever hears my word and believes Him who sent me has eternal life. He does not come into judgment, but has passed from death to life."

Would you like to know how you can receive this gift of eternal life that Jesus mentions? Here is how.

Salvation removes our FAILURE. *Jesus focuses on judgment and death.*

God created a perfect world. Adam and Eve rejected Him and chose sin bringing pain and death into the world. That sin nature was passed down to us, separating us from God and condemning us to hell. The good news is that God offers us salvation.

Salvation comes through FAITH. *Jesus says we must believe.*

Salvation is not a reward for hard work or good deeds. The Bible says we receive eternal life by turning from sin and placing our faith in Jesus.

Salvation brings FREEDOM. *Jesus says we do not come into judgment.*

Salvation satisfies the judgment our sin deserves because Jesus died in our place on the cross. His resurrection proves His power over death and the grave. Believers in Jesus are freed from an eternity in hell.

Salvation lasts FOREVER. *Jesus calls this blessing, "Eternal Life."'*

His forgiveness includes all past and future sins. He prepares a place for us in heaven. He promises you eternal life today if you repent and believe.

2

NOTES ON THE PRESENTATION

It is helpful to commit this presentation to memory for the sake of familiarity, but it should not be quoted as a one-sided monologue. Sharing the gospel is a dialogue, an exchange of ideas, with another person. This is a guided conversation that involves both the witness and the hearer. The presentation is designed to reveal the truths in the verse. So ask questions to gauge the hearer's comprehension and interest. In most situations, the hearer should be speaking more than the witness.

STATEMENT ONE: *Salvation is needed because of FAILURE. God created a perfect world. Adam and Eve rejected Him and chose sin bringing pain, and death into the world. That sin nature was then passed down and separated us from God and condemns us to hell. The good news is that God offers us salvation.*

The presentation begins with God's intentions for humanity and ends with His gracious salvation offer. Note the fact that He created all things good, but our rejection altered creation. Ultimately, our rebellion and sin introduced death and hardship into the world.

Next lead a brief discussion on "sin." The hearer must understand that sin is more than just being "bad"; it is deadly and condemned by God because of His holiness. Typically, the hearer will offer examples of sin but not a true definition. Be ready to explain that sin is a spiritual deficiency found within everyone that renders us unable to be righteous in person and in deed. It brings about alienation from God, humanity, and ourselves.

Also, explain that sin is universal; everyone is a sinner. We inherited a sinful nature from our parents following an unbroken line back to Adam and Eve. God condemns sin… all sin.

> **Possible Questions:**
> What examples of brokenness do you see around you? How do you deal with it?
> What does the word "sin" bring to mind?
> What is God's view of sin? Why does He hate it?

Transition to the second statement: As much as God hates sin, He loves us. That is why He offers salvation as a gift.

STATEMENT TWO: *Salvation comes through FAITH. It is not a reward for hard work or good deeds. The Bible says we receive eternal life by turning from sin and placing our trust in Jesus.*

The second statement contrasts faith and works. If good works could save us, they would be an occasion for us to be praised rather than God. Good deeds only impact this moment in time. They do not have the power to alter the past. They cannot remove guilt or responsibility for our wrongs.

Faith is expressing trust in the goodness of God. While it sounds simple, it is actually difficult due to our pride. We want recognition. We want to chart our own course. God calls us to surrender to His authority over us.

Possible Questions
Do you struggle with pride?
Why are "hard work and good deeds" not enough to save us?
What does Jesus mean by "believe in Him"?

Transition to the third statement: Guilt and pain can be a burden, but salvation removes them.

STATEMENT THREE: *Salvation Brings FREEDOM. It removes the judgment our sin deserves because Jesus died in our place on the cross. His resurrection proves His power over death and the grave. Believers in Jesus are freed from an eternity in hell.*

This is the heart of the presentation. It teaches the importance of Jesus' substitution. Assure them that salvation is freedom from judgment. The believer no longer fears spending eternity in hell. It is freedom from guilt. It is a fresh start with God.

The gospel's genius is that God's holiness is satisfied by Jesus' sacrifice, and His love is satisfied through our forgiveness. Jesus is God, who, in the form of a man, lived a sinless life. He willingly took our place on the cross. He suffered punishment for our sins. He rose three days later, conquering death and the grave.

Possible Questions
How do you deal with guilt or disappointment?
What makes Jesus different from other religious people?
Why is the death and resurrection of Jesus important?

Transition to the fourth statement: Jesus' promise is lasting.

STATEMENT FOUR: *Salvation lasts FOREVER. His forgiveness includes past and future sins. He prepares a place for us in heaven. He promises you eternal life today if you repent and believe.*

Share with a smile. You are communicating the joy of new life. You can assure the hearer that God is faithful to honor His word. Convey to them that salvation is not a license to sin but is freedom from the fear of God abandoning us when we do sin. Just as Jesus was victorious over sin, He provides us the power to resist the temptation to sin.

Eternal Life is almost always spoken in the Bible of as a possession in the Bible. It is not something we need to worry about receiving at the end of our life. It is a gift received at the moment we repent and place our faith in Jesus.

Possible Questions
Have you ever wondered if God loves you?
Has anyone ever betrayed you or failed to
honor a promise?
Would you like to know for sure that God is
pleased with you and accepts you into His
family forever?

CONCLUDING THE CONVERSATION:
Depending upon the hearer's response, there are several
possible directions for the conversation.

It may be appropriate to share your salvation
testimony.
You may need to address additional questions.
You may be able to lead them in prayer for
salvation.

Should the hearer place their faith in Christ, help them
understand how they should grow in their new life.
Encourage them in the spiritual disciplines, the
importance of having a church family, and the need to
tell others of their new relationship with the Lord.

3

LIFESTYLE EVANGELISM

One of the great tragedies of the church, at least in North America, is the mistaken idea that personal evangelism is a calling for only a select few. The belief is that these certain people have the spiritual gift of evangelism. They may hold a ministry position that requires them to be witnesses or have an outgoing personality. There is an actual "office of an evangelist" described in scripture (Ephesians 4:11), which is tasked with equipping believers, but there is not a gift of evangelism listed in the New Testament. Someone may be described as a "people person," but every believer has the responsibility to be a witness for Christ (Matthew 28:19-20, Acts 1:8).

Lifestyle evangelism grows out of three foundational elements. The first is the commitment to be a witness. This means we have a conviction that people bound in sin need to have the opportunity to hear and respond to the gospel. It is a sincere love for people created by God. It is the desire for them to know Him personally. This conviction stirs us to action.

The second element of lifestyle evangelism is preparation for it by learning how to share your faith. It is true that if you know enough to be saved then you know enough to lead someone else to salvation. But, scripture tells us to be prepared to share the gospel with others. That means we anticipate their potential questions and reasons for rejecting the gospel (1 Peter 3:15). The need for us to be equipped is the motivation behind this book and the SHARE! Strategy.

The assumption is that if you are reading this book, the first two elements are important to you. You want to be an effective witness, and you are seeking training. That leads to the third foundational element: how do you become a consistent witness? How do you find opportunities to share the gospel?

Ministry involvement with a local church will put believers in a position to connect with people who need the gospel. But faithful witnesses will also proclaim the gospel outside of church events. Being a witness should be a core aspect of our lives. It should be a "lifestyle" that flows out of authentic love and a sincere concern for others.

One particular tool, or spiritual discipline, draws people together and provides opportunities to present the gospel. That tool is prayer. Praying FOR people and praying WITH people can unite lives together.

One simple question, "How may I pray for you?" can open the door to a relationship. It provides a platform from which the gospel presentation can be offered. It is a question that can be asked of close friends and family members. It can be asked of co-workers, neighbors, acquaintances, and strangers. Even in a highly secular society, the question is non-threatening. A brief interaction in a department store or restaurant can become a witnessing opportunity when this question is asked.

The following are possible steps to initiate a conversation that is directed toward sharing the gospel.

1. There is an initial interaction where you connect with the other person. The conversation may have no spiritual content, but it can lead to the witness asking the question, "how may I pray for you"?

2. Some will be dismissive, some will offer vague generalities, but others will share important needs. Listen with sincerity. Seek an understanding of how these needs may be impacting them personally.

3. Take a moment and pray for them. If it is appropriate, assure them that you will continue to pray for them at a later time.

4. The conversation can turn toward an evangelistic presentation with an additional question, "Considering what you are dealing with, what gives you hope?" The witness can now ask, with a smile, "Can I tell you what gives me hope?"

5. This would begin the SHARE! presentation.

These steps are offered as a general guide. Every conversation is different and follows its own course as people interact. Not every conversation or interaction is conducive to a presentation. But if it is, this guide offers an easily reproducible strategy to follow: may I pray for you? Where does your hope come from? May I tell you where I find hope? When we sincerely care for people, they sense it and allow us to share with them.

4

OPEN-ENDED QUESTIONS TO INITIATE GOSPEL CONVERSATIONS

An abrupt presentation of the gospel to a stranger will rarely bear the fruit of salvation. The norm is that gospel conversations will arise out of life issues when two people are already connected through a relationship. That relationship may be with friends and family, or co-workers or neighbors. In general, when a believer is connected to a person, they intentionally seek opportunities to lead the person to salvation.

Below are a few examples of questions designed to steer a conversation toward the gospel. These questions, when asked by the witness provide an opportunity for their friend to express where they are spiritually. The questions also allow the witness an opportunity to clarify matters important to salvation. These are conversation starters, not points of debate. The witness may use one, several, all, or none of the questions over the course of the conversation.

QUESTION ONE: Do you consider yourself a spiritual person? Why/why not.

Note that the word "spiritual" is being used rather than religious, saved, or Christian. Sadly, those terms have been misused, or so broadly applied, that they have little connection to their actual meaning.

Religion, the formal or outward expression of personal faith, is often seen as a negative. Even though the Bible speaks of it positively (James 1:27), many religious people do not want to be saddled with that label.

Spiritual is a broad and non-threatening term open to many interpretations. Salvation matters are spiritual matters, so the question is pointed but non-threatening. It allows the person you are speaking with to share their story without preconceived ideas distorting the narrative.

This is a good opportunity to discuss the person and knowability of God. We can help people understand that God is a person who has revealed Himself to us. He is the creator of all things. He is holy and relates to us in kindness and goodness.

QUESTION TWO: Do you consider yourself close to God? How did that happen?

Spiritual people have a foundational concept of divinity. It may line up with scripture, or it may be a skewed version of the Biblical revelation, but they do have a concept of God. This question can reveal their understanding of God's nature and their conception of revelation, sin, and salvation. It can also reveal what they believe about a personal relationship with Jesus.

As they share their story of knowing God, they are sharing their heart. Points of similarity or contrast provide an opportunity for the witness to share their own personal testimony.

This is not a religious question that initiates a debate. This is a humanity question designed to discover bridges that connect our lives.

QUESTION THREE: What is the cause of the pain and struggle in our world? How do you deal with the pain inflicted by you or upon you?

The problem of suffering is one of the greatest challenges presented to Christianity. Why God allows evil, pain, and suffering? These are not always academic challenges to biblical truth. It can be a very personal question asked by people who have been hurt by life.

A general definition of karma is that good things happen to good people; bad things happen to bad people. While most people in America do not identify as Hindus, there is an amazingly high number of people who seem to hold this belief. When tragedy comes against them, they ask themselves the question, "why?" They might respond that they are good people who do good things for others, but the pain still finds them. They unknowingly behave as though they should be immune to pain and suffering.

This is an opportunity to discuss sin and its consequences. The substitutionary sacrifice of Jesus on our behalf is the satisfaction of our sin debt. It also covers the obligation another sinner has towards us when we have been hurt. Most people cannot explain how a sin debt accrued by them, or against them, can be satisfied. We need to help them understand that only Jesus can remove sin. The reality, consequences, and satisfaction of sin's debt is a major element of any gospel presentation.

QUESTION FOUR: Do you think God is loving? Who is Jesus to you?

"God is great; God is good," is the beginning of a prayer, mostly learned as a child. It is simple, but it is true: God is both great and good. Sadly, many people do not have a benevolent understanding of God. He is the creator. He is judge and jury. He is real but always ready to discipline when we are not perfect. God's goodness, His gracious and merciful nature, is foreign to them.

Many also believe in the historical person of Jesus, but it is not a biblical understanding of Him. They believe Jesus was a good man. He was a revolutionary teacher. He was an iconoclastic leader who upset the social norm. But in their estimation, He was not divine. He did not claim to be God and did not create the religious movement that elevated Him to "god status." This non-biblical view of God and Jesus leaves people unable to experience the grace offered to them in salvation.

When we listen to people, we discover much. Their inaccurate views may be the result of extra-biblical teaching. It may be a pseudo-Christian view that they develop for themselves in response to the pain inflicted upon them by people or circumstances. Authentic conversations initiated and guided by a believer can lead to the gospel and eternal salvation.

5

HOW TO WRITE YOUR OWN TESTIMONY

Acts 22 records Paul's sharing of his testimony. He explained his life before Christ, the experience of his salvation, and the change it made in him. Your own testimony should be divided into three parts: your life before salvation, how you came to faith in Christ, and the transformation in your life since then.

Write it out. It is your story but writing it out allows you to consider the overall flow of the narrative. You can consider your verbiage and how it will be heard by someone who does not have a religious background. Writing out your story allows you to practice sharing it in a concise, 3 to 4-minute format.

KEY ELEMENTS

Life Before Christ: This section covers what your life was like before you accepted Christ. Consider the following questions:

- What were you like as a person?
- What was important to you?

• What challenges or disappointments did you face?

Discovering Christ: This section explains the steps that led to your salvation. Consider the following questions:

> • When did you first hear the gospel?
> • How did you struggle with the decision to accept Christ?
> • What led you to accept Christ?

Life Since Salvation: This section explains the transformation of your life since receiving Christ. Consider the following questions:

> • What specific changes have come about because of salvation?
> • What has changed about your motivations now that Christ is in your life?

ITEMS TO REMEMBER

An effective testimony:

> • Is concise, clear, and short
> • Focuses on the Savior rather than your sin
> • Is honest and encouraging
> • Includes scripture; your story is the vehicle to convey the gospel through scripture.

6

HOW TO PRAY FOR A LOST FRIEND

We pray for H.E.A.R.T.S. to know Jesus. This acrostic has been around for years and has been used by millions to focus their hearts on lost friends and family.

Pray for receptive HEARTS.

Luke 8:5,12 A sower went out to sow his seed. And as he sowed, some fell along the path and was trampled underfoot, and the birds of the air devoured it. [12]The ones along the path are those who have heard; then the devil comes and takes away the word from their hearts so that they may not believe and be saved.

Pray for their spiritual EYES to be open.

Matt. 13:15 'For this people's heart has grown dull, and with their ears, they can barely hear, and their eyes they have closed, lest they should see with their eyes and hear with their ears and understand with their heart and turn, and I would heal them.'

Pray for God's ATTITUDE toward sin.

John 16:8 And when he comes, he will convict the world concerning sin and righteousness and judgment…

Pray the person to be RELEASED to believe.

2 Cor.10:3-4 For though we walk in the flesh, we are not waging war according to the flesh. For the weapons of our warfare are not of the flesh but have divine power to destroy strongholds.

Pray for a TRANSFORMING life.

Rom. 12:2 I appeal to you, therefore, brothers, by the mercies of God, to present your bodies as a living sacrifice, holy and acceptable to God, which is your spiritual worship. Do not be conformed to this world, but be transformed by the renewal of your mind, that by testing you may discern what is the will of God, what is good and acceptable and perfect.

7

NEXT STEPS FOR NEW BELIEVERS

The early days following a new believer's salvation will shape their growth and maturity. The following are basic Spiritual Disciplines that, if practiced with devotion, will enhance their faith.

Engage with God's Word

Engaging with God's word is vital for new believers. The popular adage is, "the Bible is the source of our faith and practice." What we know about God we know through the scriptures. God's view of us, our needs, and how He meets those needs is recorded for us in the Bible.

Believers should schedule time every day to read the Bible and become familiar with its narrative. They should make an effort to study the scriptures regularly, twice or three times per week. They should identify a passage to read, learn its meaning, and discover how it relates to the greater narrative of scripture and its implications for their life. A believer will never outgrow their commitment to engage with God's word.

Connect Through Prayer

Prayer is talking to God. It is a time intentionally set aside for enjoying His presence. It is a time of sharing your heart with Him and experiencing His love for you. In addition to a regularly scheduled time for prayer, it should be an attitude the believer pursues throughout the day.

Praying for the needs of others is a uniquely Christ-like activity. It teaches our hearts to be concerned about others' needs. It helps us to understand their challenges. It encourages us to act on their behalf.

Praying FOR others transforms lives. Praying WITH others transforms our relationships. Taking the time to initiate prayer with someone in need, even for a few moments, lets the other person know you genuinely care. Praying regularly with other believers turns friends into family. As with Bible engagement, believers will never outgrow their commitment to prayer.

Worship and Fellowship with Others

We were made to worship God. We were made to be in community with others. These two needs are both met when we participate in corporate worship with the congregation, our family of faith. Sharing life with fellow believers is an encouragement when dealing with the struggles of our own lives.

Worship adjusts our perspective. As we focus our attention upon the Lord, we take our attention away from our life's struggles. This is not denying our needs, nor diminishing their severity, but it reminds us of the One who is more than able to address our problems and satisfy our needs.

Serve Those in Need

Ministry is the visible expression of Christ in our life. As we serve others, both inside and outside our congregation, we are bringing the love of God to bear on the lives of people in need. Jesus helped others. He met needs. He showed His love through visible, tangible actions.

Every believer is blessed with a spiritual gift at the time of their salvation. Those gifts are to be used for the benefit of others. Every believer is uniquely shaped by their past experiences, personalities, interests, and giftedness. Spiritual fulfillment is found in helping others.

Share the Gospel

If you know enough to be saved, you know enough to tell someone else how to be saved. Nothing makes a joy sweeter than sharing it with others. If you have experienced the grace of God that forgives your sin through the shed blood of His Son, it is only natural that you would want the people who mean the most to you, family and friends, to experience it as well.

Sharing means there are times when we will be asked questions we cannot answer. That prompts us to study the Bible and then follow up with answers. When we share, there are times we may feel overwhelmed. That moves us to pray for guidance and encouragement. A commitment to share the gospel will bring all of the spiritual disciplines into focus and encourage the believer's personal growth.

8

EVANGELISM GAFFES AND ERRORS

Every witness who shares the gospel has a heartfelt desire to see others come to faith in Christ. Unfortunately, witnesses can inadvertently damage their own efforts. Not taking advantage of opportunities to prepare fully can lead to miscommunication. Over eagerness can lead to hollow promises during the conversation. Below are a few examples of problems that can derail evangelistic conversations.

Do not glorify your past sins.

When you are telling your story, you will address sin. You must address the subject since we are all sinners. It is the presence and practice of sin that makes salvation imperative. Unfortunately, to picture how great the grace of God is, we can fall into the trap of glamourizing our sin. We can speak of it in almost reverential tones.

When sharing your testimony, confess to sin. Share what you feel comfortable revealing and what is appropriate for the moment and the person you are evangelizing. Be careful to keep the focus on the bondage of sin, not the temporary pleasures of sin.

Do not condemn the person or remove the hope of grace.

Jesus said God did not send Him into the world to condemn it (John 3:17a). He did not have to; the world is already condemned. Some are insulted by any critique of their behavior. They do not want to accept the truth that all are sinners. Others will hold onto the belief that their sin is too egregious for God to forgive. They believe the hurt they have caused, or the hurt that has been brought against them, is too much for the blood of Jesus to cover.

No one is beyond grace. A person's sin may be especially repulsive to us, but that only magnifies the greatness of God in His love for the person and His desire to forgive them. There is no need for them to elaborate on their sin or to explain its roots. It is best to focus on God's foreknowledge and the full extent of Christ's sin offering on Calvary.

Avoid religious or Bible terms the listener may not find familiar.

Much of the language of scripture is figurative. It is made up of words, phrases, and imagery that serves as a "short-hand" approach to conveying truth. Usually, a believer and who has been in church for a while has studied the Bible, or regularly hears sermons will understand the language's meaning. People less familiar with the church can struggle. They can misunderstand the meaning of what is being said.

Keep the terms used during the gospel presentation as simple and clear as possible. Ask the person if they understand and provide plenty of time for them to ask questions. Communication is a give-and-take of ideas. It is not a one-sided monologue that is memorized and recited. Never assume you are being understood. Allow listeners the opportunity to express their understanding during the interaction.

Do not denounce people, churches, denominations, or other religions.

We seek to lead people to salvation from sin. Your friend may be involved in a false religion, but that is just one expression of his sin. Salvation will lead to the true faith and a new life of giving God His desired worship.

Satan will attempt to derail an evangelistic event by interjecting confusion into the conversation. He may cloud the gospel presentation by having the listener ask questions that seek to compare various religions or denominations. Do not attempt to promote a particular denomination, tradition, or theological position. Keep the conversation focused on the gospel.

Do not set unrealistic expectations of the Christian life.

Too often, salvation testimonies end abruptly with a picture of problem-free living. The idea is that if you will pray this prayer, and join our church, all your monetary, vocational, or relational problems will fade away. You will never struggle. You will not suffer.

It sounds nice, but there is no Biblical support for this promise. Actually, many believers find new areas of suffering in their lives because of their commitment to Christ. We want people to embrace Jesus, and we know the power of God in our own lives. We have experienced His sovereignty over our problems and we know He will work in others' lives too. But, we do not know His compete will for their lives and how He may use struggle as a tool to shape them to look more like Christ. While we cannot promise problems will be removed, we can promise that the Lord is greater than any problem they may face.

9

A GLOSSARY FOR WITNESSES

Believe/Faith

A Definition. Faith is the conscious and intentional entrusting of one's self to God. It is more than just an optimistic approach to life that supposes circumstances will turn out well. It is a commitment to the person of God and to His word.

Salvation is by faith, depending upon Jesus' sinless life, substitutionary death, and victorious resurrection rather than the efforts of humanity to correct its own problems. Faith is creedal since it affirms objective truths. It is also a commitment of our whole person to God. In trusting God for salvation, we abandon ourselves to our creator and give up our self-reliance.

Faith is a noun, a possession, as well as a verb, an action. The verb form of "believe" denotes its impact. The objective truths of scripture have such an effect that the believer's entire person is changed. To say that one is a "believer" is to say that one's state of "being" is "lived" differently because of the truth they affirm.

Word Study. The words used for faith and believe indicate a conviction that God is faithful to honor His word.

Primary Hebrew Words

Charah is to take refuge in or entrust yourself to something. It produces peace and security since it is an expression of confidence in the Lord. (Psalm 7:1, Psalm 34:22, Isaiah 57:13)

Betach has a similar meaning. It means to trust for safety. (Deuteronomy 33:12, Psalm 4:8, Proverbs 1:33)

Primary Greek Words

Pistis (noun) is used in the New Testament 244 times. It is occasionally translated as "assurance" or "belief." (Matthew 9:22, Luke 7:50, Romans 1:17, Hebrews 11:1)

Pisteuō (verb) is used in the New Testament more than 240 times. It is to believe to the point of displaying trust. (Matthew 24:23, Luke 1:20, 1 Corinthians 11:18)

Biblical Pictures. Abraham believed God, and it was accounted to him as righteousness. Habakkuk indicates that the righteous will live by their faith, which is the source and motivation for their life. Paul assures us that we have been saved by grace through faith.

Gospel

A definition. The gospel is the summation of the Christian message of salvation that has been proclaimed to the world. It is the fulfillment of the promise made in the Garden of Eden that one man, Jesus, would come to break the power of Satan and restore mankind's relationship with God, which was severed by sin. This salvation was fulfilled in the life, death, and resurrection of Jesus and has been proclaimed through the church for 2,000 years.

The literal meaning of the gospel is "good news." It encompasses all the objective truths regarding man's fallen nature, the righteous standard of God, and the work of Christ to fulfill God's standard on behalf of fallen humanity. It is the offer of new life in Christ through repentance and faith. In the New Testament he word is connected with truth, hope, promise, and peace. (Galatians 2:5, Colossians 2:23, Ephesians 3:6, Ephesians 6:15)

More than a collection of truths that must be affirmed for salvation, the gospel is the instrument of a believer's transformation. As we acknowledge our inability to maintain righteousness apart from the all-sufficient power of God, the Holy Spirit works within us to encourage us and provide strength.

Word Study. As with several words in the New Testament, "gospel" was largely unused in the contemporary culture. Initially, it referred to the reward given to a messenger; it was later equated with the message proclaimed. When the Old Testament was

translated into the Greek language during the 2nd and
3rd centuries B.C., the word was used in 1 Samuel 31:9
to denote glad tidings of victory.

Primary Greek Word

Evangelion. Used nearly 80 times in the New
Testament, the word means good news or glad
tidings (Matthew 4:23, Romans 1:16, 2
Corinthians 2:12, 1 Peter 4:17, Revelation 14:6)

Biblical Pictures. As Jesus began His formal, earthly
ministry, He proclaimed the good news. The offer of
forgiveness and new life was received with joy. The
apostles proclaimed the same message to all peoples in
every location. The separation from God was ended;
humanity could be restored.

Grace/Mercy

A definition. Grace is the unmerited favor of God that is
bestowed, without compulsion, upon people who enjoy
His undeserved love. It is the expression of His
goodness, which is revealed through benevolent actions
directed towards His creation.

Grace is the translation of a word that literally means
"gift." It is closely related to mercy. Grace bestows
unearned blessings, and mercy withholds due
retribution. Grace is the key element of the salvation
story in that God provides salvation, temporal
blessings, and eternal security to believers in spite of
our unworthiness.

Word Study. The family of words translated 'grace' was largely unused in the first-century church's contemporary culture. The New Testament writers used the word to explain the nature of God's interaction with His people. There is not a word in Hebrew that has a direct correlation to the Greek concept of grace.

Primary Hebrew Words

Chen. An attitude of favor and benevolence. It is used nearly 70 times in the Old Testament. (Esther 2:17, Psalm 45:2, Zechariah 4:7)

Chesed is used approximately 250 times and speaks of mercy, loving-kindness, and goodness. (2 Samuel 22:26, 1 Kings 20:31, Psalm 18:25, Psalm 23:6)

Primary Greek Word

Charis. A gift bestowed, unmerited favor. The word is used over 150 times in the New Testament. (John 1:14, Acts 6:8, Romans 3:24, Ephesians 2:8, James 4:6)

Biblical Pictures. From the moment Adam and Eve sinned in the garden, humanity has benefited from God's mercy and grace. He could have immediately ended their lives, but He provided a means to have their sin forgiven, and their relationship restored. David found mercy after his affair with Bathsheba. Jesus showed grace to Paul when he forgave his persecution of the church and set him aside for ministry.

Redemption

A definition. To redeem is to pay a debt or ransom. It is how salvation is accomplished since it covers the debt owed to God for our sin's offense. The currency of exchange demanded by God is blood. It was the shed blood of Jesus on Calvary that satisfied the obligation created by our unrighteousness.

Word Study. The words for redeem are transactional in nature and point to a motivational relationship.

Primary Hebrew Word

Go' el. The word is used more than 100 times in the Old Testament. It literally means "kinsman-redeemer" pointing to a familial relationship that motivates the transaction. (Exodus 6:6, Leviticus 25:48, Ruth 3:12, Psalm 107:2, Isaiah 47:4)

Primary Greek Words

Agorazo. The root of the word is agora or 'the marketplace.' It is the picture of a transactional exchange being conducted. (Revelation 5:9)

Lutroo. To free by paying a ransom. (Luke 24:21, Titus 2:14, 1 Peter 1:18)

Biblical Pictures. The relationship between Ruth and Boaz was initially based upon the kinsman-redeemer relationship. That obligation developed into a shared love between them. When Isaiah reminds Judah of God's preserving love for them, he reminds them that

—

He gave Cush and Seba in exchange for them. (Is 43:3).

Salvation

A definition. Salvation is the ultimate blessing promised in the gospel. In basic terms, it is the reality that faith in Jesus rescues believers from eternal damnation in hell. The meaning is actually much broader than that, though. Salvation provides deliverance from the guilt associated with our past sins. It is a relief from fear and any sense of estrangement from God. It produces peace with Him and with one's self.

Salvation is understood in all three tenses of time: past, present, and future. The believer has been saved from the sin's penalty, is being saved from its power, and will be saved from its presence. It is liberation from the bondage imposed by Satan, the world system, and our own corrupted flesh. The ultimate salvation is being spared from God's holy wrath against sin and unrighteousness.

Word Study. The words used for salvation point to both deliverance and preservation. This is the true nature of salvation. More than a rescue from hell, it is a transformation from the present corruption of sin to true perfection with God.

Primary Hebrew Word

Yesha. Is to be unconfined and at ease. It is the act of being rescued from a perilous situation.

(Exodus 14:13, Deuteronomy 20:4, 1 Samuel 14:45, Psalm 51:14)

Primary Greek Word

Soteria. Preservation in the midst of, or deliverance from the presence of danger. (Luke 1:69, Acts 27:34, Romans 10:1, Hebrews 11:7)

Biblical Pictures. To spare Noah from the coming judgment, the Lord directed the building of an ark. He then enclosed Noah and his family within it to spare them from His wrath. The Lord saved Jacob's family from a coming famine and then saved them again, 400 years later, from their bondage in Egypt. Salvation is pictured in Jesus' simple invitation to Peter to follow Him. It is shown in the fantastic circumstances of Paul's conversion on the road to Damascus. The book of Revelation portrays God's final act of salvation as all of creation is remade without the influence of sin.

Sin

A Definition. Sin is a spiritual deficiency found within everyone that renders us unable to be righteous in person and in deed. It is alienation from God, humanity, and ourselves. It is a rebellion that manifests itself in non-conformity to God's law, rejection of His authority, and revulsion at His holy character.

As the nexus of our emotions, reason, and will, the human heart is the seat of sin. From that vantage point, sin can corrupt every aspect of our being. Sin can be personal or social as well as individual or corporate.

The Bible teaches that sin came into the world when Adam and Eve chose to violate God's prohibition against eating from the tree of the knowledge of good and evil. Their nature was corrupted, which was then passed on to their posterity. All of humanity is born with a sin nature that influences our thoughts and actions. Therefore, we are not sinners because we do wrong; we do wrong because we are sinners.

Word Study. Several words are translated into the English word "sin." The words of the Bible's original languages paint a broader, more detailed picture of the nature and expression of sin in our lives.

Primary Hebrew Words

Chattath is used approximately 300 times in the Old Testament. It means to err, to fail, to miss the mark. It points to a moral inability to meet the righteous standard set by God. (Genesis 4:7, Leviticus 16:30, Isaiah 30:1, Amos 5:12)

Avon is used approximately 230 times. It points to the corruption, or pollution, of the soul that leads to wickedness. It is often translated as "guilt." (Genesis 44:16, 1 Samuel 20:1, Psalm 18:23, Isaiah 27:9)

Pesha It is used more than 90 times in the Old Testament. Typically it is translated as transgression or trespass. It expresses the rebellion being waged against God. (1 Kings 8:50, Job 7:21, Psalm 19:13, Amos 3:14)

Primary Greek Words

Hamartia is used more than 40 times in the New Testament. As with the Hebrew word, "Chattath," it means to err, fail, and miss the mark. It is a moral weakness. (John 5:14, Romans 3:23, 1 Corinthians 15:34, Titus 3:11)

Paraptōma is used 19 times to designate trespass, transgression, or offense. (Matthew 6:14, Mark 11:25, Romans 4:25)

Biblical Pictures. Even in a perfect environment and a right relationship with God, Adam and Eve did not have the moral strength to resist Satan's temptation. They sinned, and every generation following them has inherited their corruption. David did not resist the temptation to watch Bathsheba. That sin led him to conspire against her husband so he could have her for himself. It led to adultery, murder, and a child's death. Peter sinned in his denial of a relationship with Jesus. Judas sinned and betrayed Jesus to the ones who sought to kill Him.

10

SCRIPTURAL FOUNDATIONS FOR THE PRESENTATION

Each element of the SHARE! presentation has biblical support. The following are a selection of verses that support the four statements.

Believers are to be evangelists:

> **Matthew 28:19-20.** Go therefore and make disciples of all nations, baptizing them in the name of the Father and of the Son and the Holy Spirit, teaching them to observe all that I have commanded you. And behold, I am with you always, to the end of the age.

> **Acts 1:8.** But you will receive power when the Holy Spirit has come upon you, and you will be my witnesses in Jerusalem and in all Judea and Samaria, and to the end of the earth.

> **1 Peter 3:15.** …but in your hearts honor Christ the Lord as holy, always being prepared to make a defense to anyone who asks you for a reason

for the hope that is in you; yet do it with gentleness and respect…

God created a perfect world:

> **Genesis 1:31.** And God saw everything that he had made, and behold, it was very good. And there was evening and there was morning, the sixth day.

> **Nehemiah 9:6.** You are the LORD, you alone. You have made heaven, the heaven of heavens, with all their host, the earth and all that is on it, the seas and all that is in them; and you preserve all of them; and the host of heaven worships you.

> **Psalm 24:1-2.** The earth is the LORD's and the fullness thereof, the world and those who dwell therein, for he has founded it upon the seas and established it upon the rivers.

> **John 1:3.** All things were made through him, and without him was not anything made that was made.

Sin brought pain, brokenness, and death into the world:

> **Psalm 51:5.** Behold, I was brought forth in iniquity, and in sin did my mother conceive me.

Jeremiah 17:9. The heart is deceitful above all things, and desperately sick; who can understand it?

Romans 3:23. …for all have sinned and fall short of the glory of God…

1 Corinthians 15:22. For as in Adam all die, so also in Christ shall all be made alive.

The good news is God offers us salvation:

Jeremiah 29:13-14. You will seek me and find me, when you seek me with all your heart. I will be found by you, declares the LORD, and I will restore your fortunes and gather you from all the nations and all the places where I have driven you, declares the LORD, and I will bring you back to the place from which I sent you into exile.

Joel 2:32. And it shall come to pass that everyone who calls on the name of the LORD shall be saved. For in Mount Zion and in Jerusalem there shall be those who escape, as the LORD has said, and among the survivors shall be those whom the LORD calls.

John 3:16. For God so loved the world, that he gave his only Son, that whoever believes in him should not perish but have eternal life.

1 Timothy 2:3-4. This is good, and it is pleasing in the sight of God our Savior, who desires all people to be saved and to come to the knowledge of the truth.

Salvation comes through faith:

Genesis 15:6. And he believed the LORD, and he counted it to him as righteousness.

Habakkuk 2:4. Behold, his soul is puffed up; it is not upright within him, but the righteous shall live by his faith.

Romans 1:16-17. For I am not ashamed of the gospel, for it is the power of God for salvation to everyone who believes, to the Jew first and also to the Greek. For in it the righteousness of God is revealed from faith for faith, as it is written, "The righteous shall live by faith."

Ephesians 2:8. For by grace you have been saved through faith. And this is not your own doing; it is the gift of God.

Salvation is not a reward for hard work or good deeds:

Galatians 3:22. But the Scripture imprisoned everything under sin, so that the promise by faith in Jesus Christ might be given to those who believe.

Ephesians 2:9. [Salvation is] not a result of works, so that no one may boast.

2 Timothy 1:9. …who saved us and called us to a holy calling, not because of our works but because of his own purpose and grace, which he gave us in Christ Jesus before the ages began…

Titus 3:4-5. But when the goodness and loving kindness of God our Savior appeared, he saved us, not because of works done by us in righteousness, but according to his own mercy, by the washing of regeneration and renewal of the Holy Spirit…

Salvation brings freedom:

1 Corinthians 10:13. No temptation has overtaken you that is not common to man. God is faithful, and he will not let you be tempted beyond your ability, but with the temptation he will also provide the way of escape, that you may be able to endure it.

Hebrews 2:18. For because he himself has suffered when tempted, he is able to help those who are being tempted.

1 John 4:4. Little children, you are from God and have overcome them, for he who is in you is greater than he who is in the world.

Jesus promises you eternal life today.

Romans 6:8-11. Now if we have died with Christ, we believe that we will also live with him. We know that Christ, being raised from the dead, will never die again; death no longer has dominion over him. For the death he died he died to sin, once for all, but the life he lives he lives to God. So you also must consider yourselves dead to sin and alive to God in Christ Jesus.

Hebrews 10:12, 14. But when Christ had offered for all time a single sacrifice for sins, he sat down at the right hand of God. For by a single offering he has perfected for all time those who are being sanctified.

1 John 5:13. I write these things to you who believe in the name of the Son of God, that you may know that you have eternal life.

SOME CONCLUDING THOUGHTS

When I was a boy, our pastor would tell a story to illustrate a faithful witness's impact. He told of lamplighters in Victorian England. Early in the 19th century, gas street lamps were installed in London to light the city at night. They did not have an automated system to ignite the gas, so lamplighters would go through town at dusk to light them with long slender torches.

The lamplighters were inconspicuous. They did not announce their activities as they passed through a neighbourhood, but the result of their work was easily recognized. The streets were lit. People could travel through town with an elevated level of safety. As the lamplighters humbly performed their duties, the darkness was pushed back, and people could enjoy the benefits of the light.

Your life can have that same impact on the world. You can give evidence of the power of God to save and transform lives. Your words can bring light into the darkness produced by the brokenness of wrong choices and poor decisions. Your love can be an instrument of liberation for people bound up in sin. It is a high calling, but with a low threshold that makes it available for every believer. Simply commit yourself to be a faithful witness for Jesus. Love people, live the gospel, and SHARE!

www.ingramcontent.com/pod-product-compliance
Lightning Source LLC
Chambersburg PA
CBHW020608030426
42337CB00013B/1268